NOAH'S MUD
and other recipes

Marion Field and Elaine Ashmore
illustrated by Darren

Kevin
Mayhew

Acknowledgements

We would like to thank Naomi Taylor, Sophie Robson and Omar Zia for trying out the recipes for us, so this book is for them.

Authors' note: The compilers of this book have thoroughly enjoyed working on it. Elaine devised the recipes and tested them out with the children. Marion was the 'official' taster and recommends all the recipes and has also written the stories. Thanks also go to Darren for his wonderful interpretation of the whole idea.

Introduction

Hands up all those who like reading and enjoy cooking as well! Everyone? Brilliant! Then this is the book for you! Each recipe is linked to a story taken from different books in the Bible. Starting with the Flood from the Old Testament and finishing with the Easter Story in the New Testament, you will travel through the Bible and along the way enjoy lots of fun recipes and delicious food! Everything you have to do is set out very clearly, but remember not to do anything unless you have an adult to help you. And, when you have made some of these delicious treats, you can try them out on your family and friends. They will love them!

Before You Start

Are the things easy to make? To help you with this, there are stars by the recipes to show you which are very easy, easy and a little more difficult, like this:

* **Very easy**

** **Easy**

*** **Difficult**

And Remember:
1. Ask an adult to help you.
2. Put on an apron and wash your hands.
3. Get out all the things you will need for the recipe before you start.

The Flood

Many years after God had made men and women, he was angry with them because they had all become wicked and no longer listened to him. He decided to destroy the earth with an almighty flood, but save the only family who still listened to him, and two of all the creatures on the earth. This was Noah's family. Noah had a wife and three sons called Seth, Ham and Japeth, who also all had wives.

God told Noah to build a huge boat called an ark, and into this he was to take his family and all the creatures before the rain started. The ark would float and Noah, his family and all the creatures would

be saved. God showed Noah how to build the ark and when it was finished, Noah did exactly what God had told him to do; he collected two of every creature, and loaded them on to the boat.

The rain poured down for forty days and forty nights, and when at last it stopped raining and the floodwater started to go down, the ark came to rest on a mountain called Mount Ararat. They had all been saved from the flood!

Now imagine how muddy the ground must have been after all that rain and floodwater — squelchy and squishy and squodgy! This first recipe is a bit like gooey mud, but is a lot more fun because it tastes great!

NOAH'S MUD

Remember always to wash your hands
and ask an adult to help you!

Recipe Ingredients

100 grams milk or plain chocolate
1 pot 250 grams Mascarpone cheese,
which can be found in most supermarkets
8 Jaffa cakes or similar
A little orange juice to soften the cakes
Some icing sugar
4 glacé cherries

Utensils

    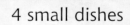

Saucepan   Pyrex dish which   Bowl   Wooden spoon   4 small dishes
            will fit over the   Dessert spoon
            saucepan

Time to Create!

1. Half fill the saucepan with water and place on cooker.

2. Break the chocolate into the Pyrex bowl and place this on top of the saucepan, making sure the water doesn't touch the bottom of the bowl.

3. Turn on the cooker hob and as the chocolate melts, stir gently with the wooden spoon.

4. When completely melted turn off the heat and, using your oven gloves, remove the Pyrex bowl from the saucepan. Ask an adult to help you.

5. Put the cheese into the bowl and mix until smooth.

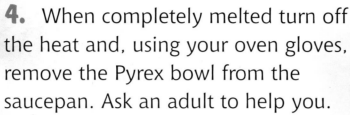

6. Add a dessertspoonful of icing sugar and mix in.

7. Add the chocolate to this and mix until it is a light chocolate colour.

8. Break two Jaffa cakes into each dish and pour a little orange juice onto each to soften them.

9. Spoon the chocolate mixture equally between the four dishes and decorate with a glacé cherry. You could also use a little whipped cream or some chocolate flakes for decoration.

Yum scrum!

Jacob and Esau

One of Noah's descendants was called Isaac. He had two sons called Esau and Jacob. They were twins but Esau was born first. In those days, being the eldest son was very important, and Jacob wished he was the elder.

One day, Jacob had just made some soup for himself. It was called pottage and was made of lentils – a sort of bean. Esau had been hunting and when he came in, he was very hungry.

'Can I have some of that pottage?' he asked. 'It smells delicious!'

Jacob thought for a moment. Then he said, 'You can have it on one condition.'

'What's that?' asked his brother, getting hungrier by the minute!

'Sell me the right to be the eldest son instead of you.'

Esau was very worried when he heard this. He knew it would not be right, but he was very, very hungry. He did not really care about being the elder brother. 'All right,' he agreed.

'You promise?' said Jacob.

'Yes!' said Esau. 'Now please give me the pottage. I'm starving.'

Jacob smiled as he handed over the food. Esau had sold his birthright for a bowl of pottage.

This recipe uses baked beans instead of lentils, and it's scrummy!

Jacob's Pottage

Recipe
Ingredients

1 onion – a red one looks really colourful.
1 tin of baked beans
Half teaspoon mixed herbs
Half teaspoon Marmite
2 teaspoonsful olive oil
Salt and pepper to taste
Sprig of parsley to decorate
2 hunks of French bread

Utensils

Saucepan   Tin opener   Spoon   Knife   Chopping board   2 bowls
                                            Wooden spoon

Time to Create!

1. Peel the onion, and chop it into small pieces. Get an adult to help you with this.

2. Put the olive oil and chopped onion into the saucepan, and turn the cooker hob on to a low heat.

LOW

3. Stir until the onion softens and add salt, pepper and herbs.

4. Now add the Marmite and mix it in.

5. Open the tin of baked beans (ask an adult to do this) and pour into the pan.

6. Keep stirring so it doesn't burn, and make sure the Pottage is heated thoroughly. Don't boil it!

7. Pour into bowls, decorate with the parsley and eat immediately with French bread.

Sensational!

Delicious!

Escape from Egypt

Pharaoh, the king of Egypt, refused to let the people of Israel leave Egypt. They had been there for a very long time and hated it. God promised to lead them out of Egypt to a country called Canaan. He told them it was 'a land flowing with milk and honey', which meant there would be plenty of food for them so they would never go hungry.

After many plagues, God finally said he would kill the eldest sons of every family in Egypt. He told the Israelites to kill a lamb and put its blood on the doors of their houses. By doing this,

their eldest sons would be safe because the Angel of Death would Pass Over them. They did as God told them and were able to escape from Egypt.

This 'Passover' is still remembered with a special meal by the Jews today. When the Israelites reached Canaan, they thanked God for leading them out of Egypt. Later they made a special food to remember that time.

'Blintzes' are a sort of pancake made with cheese and milk. This recipe is for honey pancakes to remind you of 'the land flowing with milk and honey'.

HONEY PANCAKES

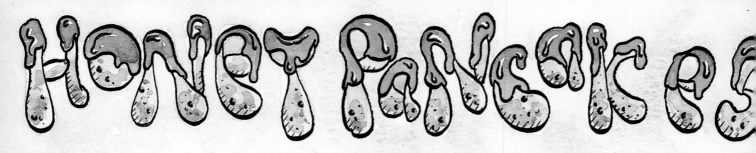

Be careful with the frying pan.

Recipe **This will make about six pancakes.**
Ingredients

$\frac{1}{2}$ pint of milk
4 ounces of plain flour
1 egg
A pinch of salt
Runny honey
A little olive oil
Slice of lemon or lime

Utensils

Small   Bowl   Wooden   Whisk   Slice   Measuring jug   Fork   Plate
frying pan   spoon

Time to Create!

1. Mix the flour and salt in the bowl, then make a hollow in the centre of the flour and break the egg into it.

2. Stir with the wooden spoon and add the milk gradually until all the flour is worked in. Beat well.

3. Put a little olive oil into the frying pan, turn on the cooker and heat the oil.

4. Pour in enough batter to cover the bottom of the pan.

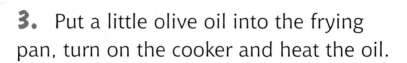

5. Check that the underneath of the pancake is brown (use the slice to do this) and carefully turn the pancake over using the slice. (If you feel adventurous, ask an adult to help and flip the pancake over in the air!)

6. When the other side is brown, lift the pancake carefully on to the plate.

7. Spoon on the honey, and decorate with the lemon or lime slice. Now eat it before someone else does!

Scrummy!

The Gifts of the King

At Christmas we remember the birthday of God's Son, Jesus. He was born in a stable in Bethlehem because there was no room in any of the inns or hotels.

After he was born, three kings from far away visited him. They brought gifts for the baby and we are told that these were gifts of gold, frankincense and myrrh. Frankincense and myrrh are spices.

The Tasty Truffles in this recipe make lovely gifts at Christmas. They look great if you present them in a small gold box, which you can buy from many gift shops. Treats fit for a king!

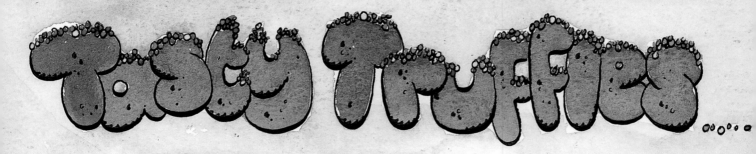

Tasty Truffles......

Eat these within ten days of making them!

Recipe
Ingredients

100 grams of plain or milk chocolate
50 grams butter
25 grams stale cake crumbs
25 grams ground almonds
220 grams sifted icing sugar
Chocolate 'Hundreds and Thousands' on a saucer.
Yolks of two eggs

Utensils

Saucepan   Pyrex bowl   Wooden   Tablespoon   Teaspoon   Knife   Plate
                            spoon

Time to Create!

1. Half fill the saucepan with cold water and put it on the cooker ready to use.

2. Break the chocolate into the Pyrex bowl and add the butter.

3. Put the Pyrex bowl on top of the saucepan, making sure that the water doesn't touch the bottom of the bowl.

4. Turn on the cooker to a medium heat and then stir the chocolate and butter with the wooden spoon as they melt.

5. Turn the heat off when the butter and chocolate have completely melted, and, using your oven gloves, carefully remove the Pyrex bowl from the saucepan. You may need an adult to help you.

6. Ask an adult to separate the egg yolks into a cup – you don't need the whites. (This is really hard, so make sure they get it right!)

7. Add the yolks to the mixture and mix thoroughly. Add the icing sugar, cake crumbs and ground almonds.

8. Now, using the teaspoon, get a heaped spoonful of the chocolate and roll it carefully into a ball. Roll it around in the 'Hundreds and Thousands'. Repeat this until there is no mixture left.

9. Put the truffles in the fridge until they are hard (about an hour and a half) and then place them in attractive foil cases. Perfect for a Christmas gift!

Mmm!

Mmm!

Jesus Calls Some Fishermen

When Jesus was older, and started to tell people about God, he needed some friends to help him with his work. One day as he was walking beside the Sea of Galilee, he saw some fishing boats. Two fishermen were throwing their nets into the sea to catch the fish. They were brothers called Peter and Andrew.

Jesus watched them for a little while and then he called out to them. 'Come with me!' he shouted.

Peter and Andrew looked up and immediately got out of their boat and went wading through the water and along the shore to Jesus.

A little further on they saw another boat, and in it were two brothers called James and John, who were mending their nets. When Jesus called out to them, they also followed him.

What better way to remind ourselves of these fishermen who followed Jesus, than to make something delicious with fish!

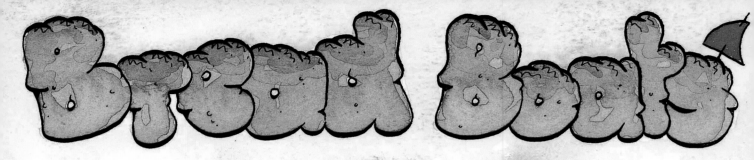

Bread Boats

Try different fillings, such as salmon or even sardines!

Recipe
Ingredients

Two long bread rolls
Tin of tuna
Mayonnaise
Salt and pepper to taste
A squeeze of lemon juice
Packet of crisps

Utensils

Bread knife   Bowl   Chopping board   Tablespoon   Plate   Coloured   Cocktail
Tin opener   Wooden spoon   sticky   sticks
                                                                    paper

Time to Create!

1. Carefully cut off the tops of the bread rolls.

2. Scoop out the bread with your fingers and place in the bowl, tearing it into small pieces.

3. Get an adult to open the tin of tuna, drain off the juice and then add the tuna to the bread.

4. Add a tablespoonful of mayonnaise (more if you want to), a little salt, pepper and a squeeze of lemon to taste. Mix well.

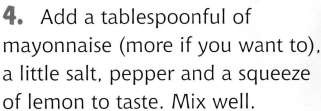

5. Spoon the mixture into the bread 'boats', and sprinkle the crushed crisps on top.

6. To make the sail:
a Fold a square of coloured paper into a triangle and stick together.
b Carefully make two holes at the side with the cocktail stick – ask an adult to help you.
c Push the cocktail stick through the holes and stick the 'sail' into the 'boat'.

7. Arrange the 'boats' on a plate and eat right away!

Fantastic!

The Parable of the Sower

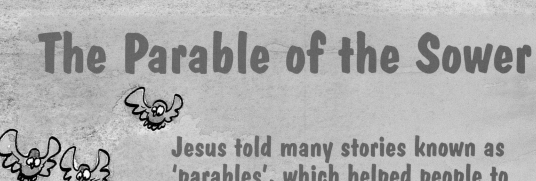

Jesus told many stories known as 'parables', which helped people to understand what he was saying. One day, he told this story about a farmer sowing his corn in his field. Some of the seed fell on the path so the birds ate it. Some fell on stony ground so the seeds could not go deep into the earth. The corn grew quickly but when the sun came out it burnt the young plants and they died. Some seed was choked by weeds so it could not grow properly. But some seed fell on the good soil. This grew quickly and the farmer had a great deal of corn. 'What does the story mean?' someone asked Jesus, when he had finished. Jesus told them that the story was about four types of

people. The seed was the Word of God. The first seeds that were eaten by the birds were the people who listened to God but did not try to understand. The seeds that fell on the stony ground were those people who listened to God and believed what he told them, but soon forgot what he had said. The seeds choked by the weeds were the people who were too busy to listen to God.

Jesus told the people to be like the 'good soil'. They should listen to what God tells them and not let other things distract them. He wants us to listen to him too.

This recipe represents the 'Stony Path'. God doesn't want us to be like this, but to listen to him and love him as he loves us.

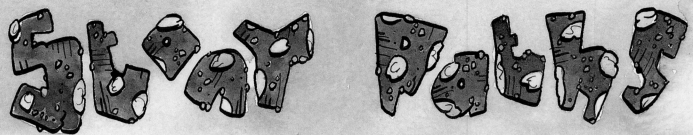

Stony Paths

Recipe

The marshmallows make tasty stones!

Ingredients

100 grams milk chocolate
100 grams plain chocolate
100 grams tiny multicoloured marshmallows.
(You can find these at the baking section in most supermarkets, or instead, just cut up bigger ones!)
Half a packet of Rich Tea biscuits
1 dessertspoonful of cooking oil
A little butter

Utensils

Small piece of greaseproof paper Small, square cake tin	Wooden spoon Dessert spoon	Saucepan	Pyrex dish	Oven gloves	Plastic food bag	Rolling p

Time to Create!

1. Put the biscuits in the food bag and carefully break them with the rolling pin. Ask an adult for help.

2. Spread the butter over the bottom of the cake tin, using the greaseproof paper.

3. Half fill the saucepan with water and put on the cooker ready to use.

4. Break the chocolate into the Pyrex bowl and add the cooking oil to the chocolate.

5. Put the Pyrex bowl on top of the saucepan, making sure the water doesn't touch the bottom of the bowl.

6. Gently heat, and as the chocolate melts, stir gently with the wooden spoon. Turn the heat off when completely melted.

7. Using your oven gloves and, asking an adult to help, carefully remove the Pyrex bowl from the saucepan and put some of the chocolate into the baking tin.

8. Dot the marshmallows and broken biscuits all over this chocolate. Now pour the rest of the chocolate mixture on top.

9. Allow to cool and then place in the fridge until hard.

10. Cut into squares and gobble up with family and friends!

Super!

Urp!

The Easter Story

Remember the Passover Meal, earlier in the book? As a child, Jesus had gone to Jerusalem with his parents to celebrate this festival. He also went with his friends when he was older, but one year it was different because he knew he was going to die.

The 'Passover Meal' that he shared with his disciples that night, we now call 'The Last Supper'. During the meal, Jesus gave bread and wine to his friends, and we remember this when we take the bread and wine in church. We call this a number of names such as Communion, the Eucharist, the Lord's Supper or the Breaking of Bread.

After the meal was over, Judas, one of the twelve disciples, betrayed Jesus and turned him over to some soldiers who took him away. Some people hated Jesus because they were afraid of him, and eventually Jesus was crucified. This means he hung on a cross until he died. He was then put in a tomb with a huge stone in front of the entrance.

After three days, the stone was rolled away and Jesus walked from the tomb – alive! And he is still alive today!

At Easter, we eat Easter eggs, which can help us to remember the stone that was rolled away from the tomb. In some places, the custom is to decorate eggs and roll them down a hill, just like the rolling stone.

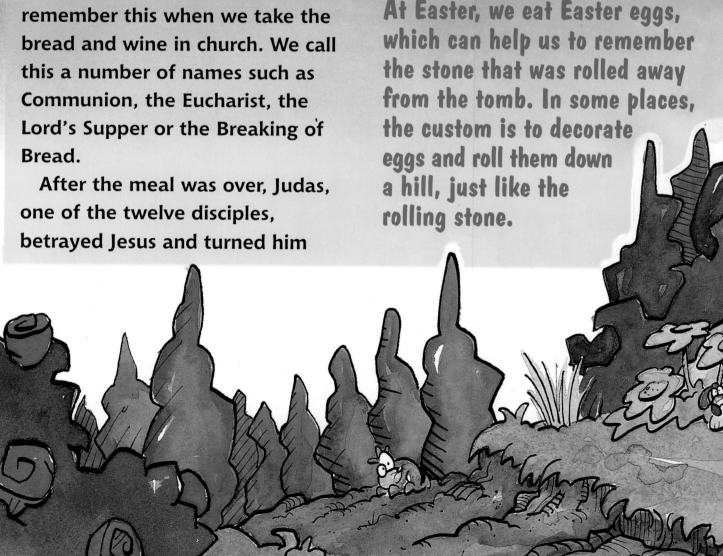

Exciting Easter Eggs

Great for breakfast at Easter!

Recipe
Ingredients

Four eggs
Water
Food colouring – red and green
Tea bags

Utensils

Saucepan   Tablespoon   Teaspoon   Bowl   Coloured felt-tipped pens

Time to Create!

To Make Coloured and Decorated Eggs:

1. Place two eggs into a saucepan of cold water and add two teaspoonsful of food colour. (Red looks great!)

2. Turn on the cooker, bring the water to the boil and gently boil the eggs for ten minutes.

3. Turn off the heat and remove the saucepan from the cooker.

4. Take the eggs out of the water using the tablespoon – ask an adult to help – and place in a bowl of cold water.

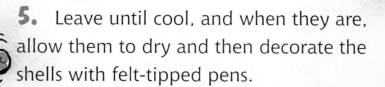

5. Leave until cool, and when they are, allow them to dry and then decorate the shells with felt-tipped pens.

To Make a Very Ancient-Looking Egg:

1. Hard boil the eggs as before, but in plain water.

2. When cool, crack the shell by tapping it gently with a teaspoon, but do not remove it!

3. Put cold water in a saucepan with two tea bags, put on the cooker and bring to the boil.

4. Using the tablespoon, lift the cracked eggs into the water and gently boil for ten minutes.

5. Turn the heat off, remove the saucepan and remove the eggs as before, placing into cold water.

6. When cool, remove the shell and you have an ancient-looking egg, all cracked and brown! Instead of using tea bags, you can use the food colouring which will make some really cool patterned, colourful eggs!

Cool!

First published in 1998 by
KEVIN MAYHEW LTD
Rattlesden
Bury St Edmunds
Suffolk IP30 0SZ

0 1 2 3 4 5 6 7 8 9

ISBN 1 84003 181 6
Catalogue No 1500186

Front cover and illustrations by Darren
Art Direction by Jaquetta Sergeant
Edited by David Gatward
Printed in Great Britain